JohnnyCash

text **Paula Taylor**
illustrations **John Keely**
design concept **Mark Landkamer**

published by **Creative Education
Mankato, Minnesota**

Published by Creative Educational Society, Inc.,
123 South Broad Street, Mankato, Minnesota 56001
Copyright © 1975 by Creative Educational Society, Inc. International copyrights reserved in all countries.
No part of this book may be reproduced in any form without written permission from the publisher. Printed in the United States.
Distributed by Childrens Press, 1224 West Van Buren Street, Chicago, Illinois 60607
Library of Congress Number: 74-14549   ISBN: 0-87191-391-7

Library of Congress Cataloging in Publication Data
Taylor, Paula.   Johnny Cash.
SUMMARY: A brief biography emphasizing the career of the singer whose songs often express his concern for "poor and forgotten people."
1. Cash, Johnny—Juvenile lit. [1. Cash, Johnny. 2. Singers, American]
I. Keely, John, illus. II. Title.
ML3930.C27T4   784'.092'4 [B] [92]   74-14549
ISBN 0-87191-391-7

U. S. 1837535

In Concert

Two thousand inmates in their denim uniforms march single file into the prison cafeteria. They sit down on the hard benches. Up above on the catwalks, guards with shotguns pace watchfully back and forth. A cell door clangs shut. At last the man they're all waiting for strides out onto the makeshift stage, his guitar slung around his neck. He's 6 feet tall, lanky, and dressed all in black. His haggard, scarred face wears a mournful expression. "Hello," he says simply. "I'm Johnny Cash."

As thunderous applause explodes around him, Cash swings into "Folsom Prison Blues."

"I'm stuck in Folsom Prison
And time keeps draggin' on."

Cash goes on singing. He gives voice to the prisoners' fears and anger, their hopes and dreams. He sings of the frustration of sitting day after day staring at a wall, of the loneliness of being separated from home and family, of the longing to get outside the walls.

Last of all Johnny Cash announces a song written by one of the prisoners. Cash looks down at him and says, "I hope I do your song justice, friend." He starts singing: "Inside the walls of a prison my body may be; but the Lord has set my soul free." Two thousand convicts rise to their feet, honoring the man who wrote the song. As the last notes fade away, the men whistle, cheer, clap, and shout their thanks to Johnny Cash.

Later millions of people across the nation heard the laughter and applause of the convicts, as well as the clanging of cell doors, the shriek of sirens, and the shouts of the guards. Johnny Cash's performance had been recorded live at Folsom Prison.

Audiences

Prisoners aren't the only ones who applaud Johnny Cash. Every year at state fairs across the land, sunburned farmers and middle-aged ladies in neat print dresses sit for hours in the hot sun to get the best seats for the evening performance.

When Johnny Cash appeared at Carnegie Hall, men and women in formal attire applauded him just as enthusiastically. At the White House dignitaries found themselves tapping their feet in time to his music.

Even after playing at Carnegie Hall and the White House, Johnny Cash still insists, "Convicts are the best audience I ever played for."

Bob Johnston, who recorded Cash's performance at Folsom, explains the enthusiastic reaction of the prison audience this way: "John went in there believing in what he was doing. He had a lot of love and compassion, and they gave it back to him. You can't buy that."

For 6 years Cash had prodded producers at Columbia to let him record one of his performances at Folsom Prison. "I thought it would be a big album for me," he says, "but my motives were not money ... I thought people would take notice of men that have been forgotten in everybody's mind."

Cash has always been concerned about the people many of us tend to forget. Long before others recognized the problem, Johnny Cash was protesting the treatment of native Americans. He himself is proud of his Cherokee ancestry.

One of the songs on the album, the "Ballad of Ira Hayes," made a lot of people uneasy. The song recounts the true story of the Indian Marine who raised the American flag on Iwo Jima in the thick of a fierce battle in World War II. Years later Ira Hayes died, drunk and

penniless in a ditch, his bravery unremembered.

Many people thought country singers shouldn't get involved in the problems of Indians. Some members of the Country Music Association demanded that Cash resign. Disc jockeys refused to play "Ira Hayes." But Johnny Cash kept on singing the song.

He kept on singing at prisons, too, even when many of his fans criticized him for it. And he did more than just entertain the men. When he played at Arkansas' brutal Cummins Prison Farm, some members of the State Legislature were touring the prison. Seeing them in the audience, John belted out a song he'd composed for the occasion: "There's a lot of things need changin', Mr. Legislature Man." Three weeks later the Legislature voted the first tax money ever spent in Arkansas for prison improvement.

Johnny Cash usually gets thousands of dollars for a performance, but often he plays free to benefit a cause he believes in. Once he turned down a $10,000 television appearance in England so he could do a free show for Indians on the Rosebud Reservation in South Dakota. Georgia prison officials offered him $5,000 for an appearance. He wrote back that he wouldn't sing for $5,000, but he'd come and sing for free if they'd use the $5,000 for the men.

Flashback

Perhaps Johnny Cash's sympathy for poor and forgotten people comes from his memories of his own childhood. He was born during the depression. His father had been a farmer, but in 1932 cotton prices were down to almost nothing in southern Arkansas. Ray Cash worked at whatever jobs were available for as little as 25 cents a day.

In 1935 the Cashes were among 500 families chosen to move to Dyess Colony in northern Arkansas. The government issued them a mule, a cow, a house, and 20 acres of land to help them get a new start. They were to pay back the loan year by year as the crops came in. The new land was rich, but life wasn't easy for Carrie and Ray Cash and their 5 children. Stumps had to be dug out, snakes killed, cotton planted and picked. Everyone worked, even 4-year-old John.

Two years after the Cashes moved to Dyess, there was a disastrous flood. As the water surged higher and higher, families left their homes to find safety on higher ground. Some didn't come back. The Cashes did. They cleared out the mud and started over again.

Gradually, the farm began to prosper. Carrie Cash sent away for a radio. Soon young John was spending every spare moment listening to country music.

Life was slow and simple in Dyess. But the radio gave young John Cash a glimpse of the world outside of Dyess. "I'd listen to all those country music programs: The Carter Family, The Browns, Ferry Four. Every Saturday night there would be the Grand Ole Opry from WSM in Nashville."

John began dreaming of becoming a country singer. His mother, the daughter of a singing teacher, was determined that John should have voice lessons. She took in washing and ironing to get the 50 cents to pay for his first lesson. After a month his teacher told him not to change the way he sang. She confessed to his mother that his voice was so unique there wasn't much she could teach him.

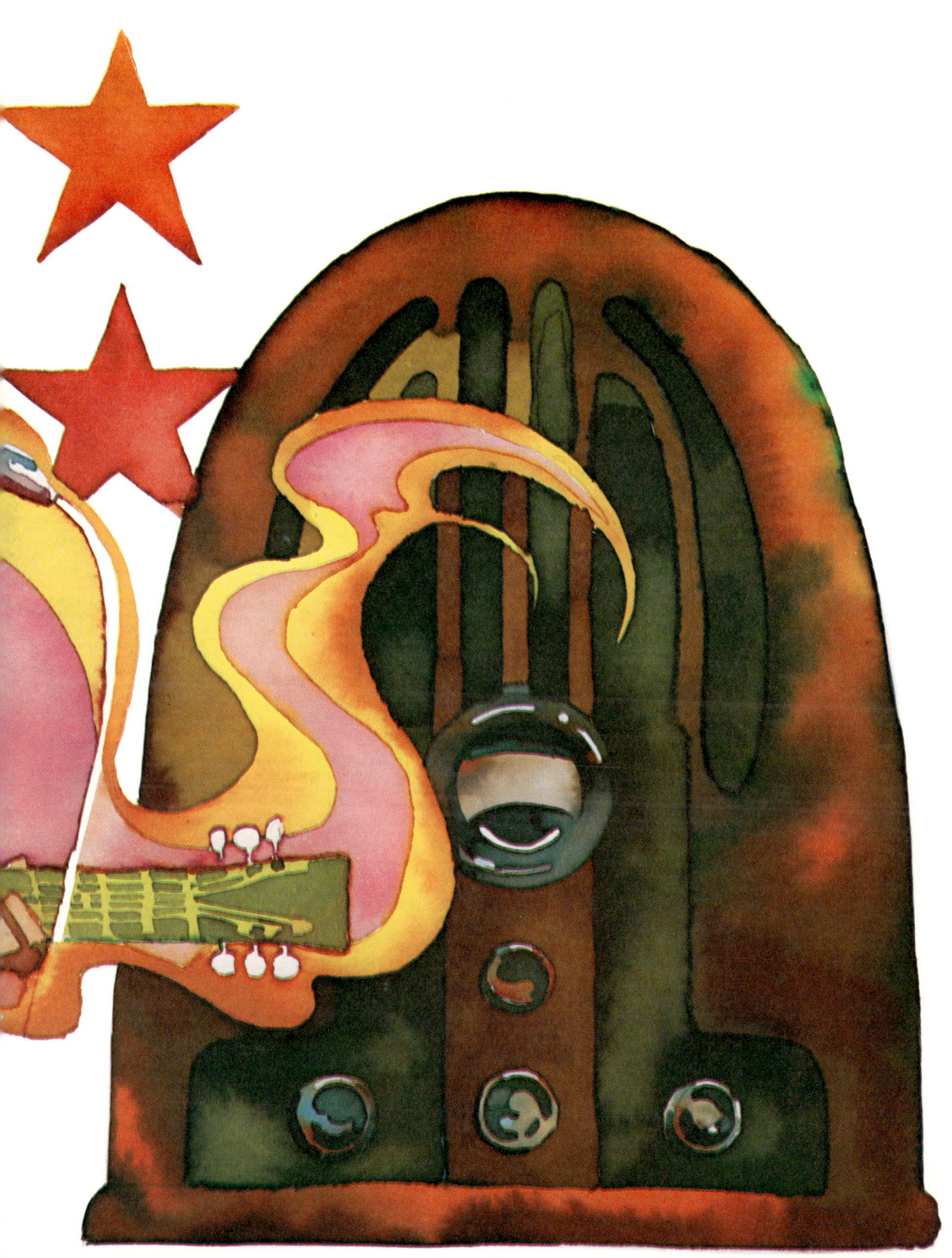

As John grew older, he became an expert at picking cotton and doing other farm chores. However, sometimes his love of music interfered with his work. When he was 16, his father got him a job on a local work project. The men were clearing brush along the Tyronza River. John was to be the water boy. He had to fill two 5-gallon cans with water from the nearest farm pump and lug the eighty-pound load back to the workers. On the way he passed a car belonging to one of the men. The temptation was too much. He got into the car, turned on the radio, and happily listened to one country music program after another.

Back at the river, the men began grumbling. They were thirsty and angry. When they finally located John, the car battery had gone dead. The next day the workers had a new water boy.

John's later work experience was equally unpromising. After he graduated from high school, he took a bus to Detroit. He got a job in the Fisher Body plant but was lonely and didn't like the work. In 2 weeks he was back home. A job in an oleomargarine factory also lasted 2 weeks. Finally he enlisted in the Air Force.

"In the Air Force was where I started finding myself," Cash now says. "I was proud of the work I was doing because I excelled in it." He became a radio operator.

Because John picked up Morse code so fast, he was one of the few men chosen to train for the difficult job of monitoring international flight traffic. At the end of the course, Cash was sent to Landsberg, Germany. While on duty, he sat with earphones on 8 hours a day, locating and copying the coded ground and air traffic of the Soviet Air Force. He was assigned to more and more difficult jobs.

In the barracks he met other country music buffs. Some played the guitar and sang. John bought a German guitar. His friends helped him learn the chords. They formed their own group, the "Landsberg Barbarians."

By the time he had finished his tour of duty, John was not only singing and playing the guitar, but also writing songs. John Cash had to find out whether he could make a living playing country music.

After he was discharged, Cash went to Memphis to visit his brother Roy. Hoping he might be able to get into the music business as a disc jockey, John signed up for a course in radio announcing. However he couldn't study full-time. He was going to get married to Vivian Liberto, a girl he'd met before he was sent to Germany. Roy Cash heard that an appliance company needed a salesman. John applied and got the job.

He quickly found he was no salesman. "I hated trying to convince people they should have something they didn't really want," Cash recalls. "I felt dishonest." Cash's love of music also took his mind off his job. He recalls, "I'd be in a home and I'd see a guitar, and I'd sit and play and forget the whole business."

On Record

John's brother Roy was a service manager at a garage. One day he took John over to the shop to meet 2 of the mechanics, Marshall Grant and Luther Perkins. They also played the guitar. Soon John was stopping by the garage every night after work.

One night Cash suggested that they try playing different instruments. Luther borrowed an electric guitar. Marshall borrowed a bass. Nobody knew how to play

the bass. Luther played notes one by one on his guitar, and they marked them on the bass with adhesive tape. They spent long hours practicing. Soon they were giving free shows, playing gospel songs at church barbeques.

John convinced Marshall and Luther that they should try to make a record. They decided Sun Records was the place to go. The owner, Sam Phillips, had discovered Elvis Presley and other promising young singers. Maybe he'd give them a chance.

Phillips agreed to the audition. However, after hearing them play, he said he was sorry. There just wasn't any market for gospel. The trend was toward rock 'n' roll. Hesitantly, Cash said he could do a song like that—one he'd written in the Air Force called "Hey, Porter." He ran through the song. Phillips liked it. If Cash could come up with another like it for the flip side, he'd make the record.

Excited, John went home and started working on another song. After two weeks, "Cry, Cry, Cry" was finished. Cash called Sam Phillips for another audition. Phillips was busy. It was 2 months before he had time to listen to them again.

During that time the group began experimenting, trying to come up with a sound that would intrigue Phillips. Cash stuck a piece of paper between his guitar strings and the neck frets. When he played, the paper rattled, sounding like brushes on a snare drum. Luther tried a new way of playing his guitar, and Marshall bought an electric amplifier.

Finally a date was set for the second audition in the tiny, cluttered Sun studio. Sam Phillips liked "Cry, Cry, Cry." He wanted to make the record right away. Cash and his friends were nervous. They were having trouble

adjusting the new amplifier. Luther had not quite mastered the new method of guitar picking. Marshall wasn't quite sure of some of the notes on his bass. They tried "Cry, Cry, Cry" 35 times before Phillips was satisfied; but at the end of the session, they had a record.

The next day Phillips called to ask what they wanted to name the group. Cash suggested "The Tennessee Three." Marshall objected. Since Cash would be doing all the singing, he reasoned, it ought to be "John Cash and the Tennessee Two." Phillips thought "*Johnny* Cash and the Tennesee Two" would appeal to the teen-agers, who were buying most of the single records.

They agreed on the name, and Johnny Cash signed the recording contract for the group. When he walked out, he had just 15 cents in his pocket. On the way home, he gave that away to an old man who asked him for money.

It was another 2 months before the record was released. One April morning while Marshall was driving to work, half-listening to the music on the radio, he heard the disc jockey say, "I got a new record here on the Sun label, and it's a gas." It was "Cry, Cry, Cry." "I don't know these boys," said the disc jockey when the song ended, "but I've never heard anything come in with such a different sound. It won't be the last time you hear of them."

The record sold over 100,000 copies, and bookings started turning up around Memphis and sometimes as far away as Arkansas and Mississippi. They played at high school auditoriums, movie theatres and ball parks. Usually the money just about paid for the gas. They would have made more playing in bars; but Johnny refused to play where liquor was served, even though he needed the money badly. Today Cash says, "Those shows aren't pleasant memories. They're not the good old days to me." But it was on cramped stages with faulty microphones and poor lighting that Johnny Cash became a pro.

Eventually Cash's group began touring with other country performers including Elvis Presley. The pay rose to $100 a night, but the tours stretched from Georgia to Colorado with hundreds of miles between stops. The pace was exhausting, but the long days of driving gave Cash time to write his songs. He would pick up a scrap

On Tour

of paper and jot down a few guitar chords or runs and a few words. Then he'd stuff the paper into his pocket. Weeks later he'd come across it again and work on it some more. After more than 500 songs, he still works this way.

Cash's first big hit, "I Walk the Line," actually resulted from a mistake. Some of his Air Force buddies were fooling around with their guitars while Johnny was at work. They borrowed his tape recorder and taped the session. Somehow they accidentally rewound the tape backwards. Later when Cash turned on his recorder, he heard a haunting melody. He couldn't figure out how it had gotten on his tape or what it was. But he couldn't get the tune out of his mind. "I just started practicing those guitar runs," he says. "At the end of each run, I started saying, 'Because you're mine, I walk the line.'"

Eventually Johnny figured out what had happened to the tape, but the melody still intrigued him. Years later when the group was touring in Texas, the rest of the song came to him all at once one night in a motel room. It became a smash hit, selling over 2 million copies, and brought Cash a television appearance on The Jackie Gleason Show. Soon Johnny Cash and the Tennessee Two were performing nation-wide.

In Trouble

Johnny Cash seemed to have reached the pinnacle of success. He had millions of records and thousands of concerts to his credit. However the life of a country singer wasn't easy. Road trips became even longer and more hectic. The tension of performing on a tight schedule was wearing.

With Marshall and Luther as willing accomplices, Johnny started playing practical jokes for diversion. He would bring an aerosol can of shaving cream along to a restaurant, sneak a pie off the shelf, decorate it with cream, and set it back on the shelf.

In time their high-jinks became more destructive. They would get cans of black, green, orange and red paint and paint each wall of a motel room a different color. Cash always paid the bills for the damage, but their jokes began giving all country musicians a bad name. Hotels refused to rent rooms to them.

By 1961 Johnny Cash was giving 290 shows a year and driving 300,000 miles in the process. When he wasn't on the road, he was making records for Columbia, which had bought his contract from Sun Records. He had moved his wife and 4 young daughters to a new home in California but was rarely able to spend time with them.

As the strain and fatigue increased, Cash started taking pep pills or amphetamines. At that time few doctors were aware of how dangerous the pills were. Cash had no trouble getting prescriptions for them. He first started taking the pills to overcome the shyness he still felt every time he went on stage. Then as the hectic pace increased, he took them so he could stay up late at night to work on the songs he was writing.

It wasn't unusual for the group to do a show one night, then pack up and drive all the next day to make an evening performance in another city 800 miles away. Cash would take pills to stay awake on the road. Then he would take more to make sure he was alert for the performance. By the time the show was over, he'd have to take tranquilizers to get to sleep. Then he'd take more pep pills to wake up again. Little by little, his tolerance

increased, until he was taking up to 100 pills a day. The more amphetamines he took to go "up," the more tranquilizers he needed to come back "down."

During the next 7 years, Cash took more and more pills. He began eating less and sleeping less. Sometimes he had voice trouble. But no matter how terrible he felt, he was usually able to pull himself together for a performance.

When he was on stage, Johnny Cash's personal warmth and magnetism were as compelling as ever. Audiences grew bigger and bigger. One of his friends remarked in amazement after Cash's performance at the Hollywood Bowl, "He would hardly even croak, and he had them eating out of the palm of his hand."

June Carter joined the Cash troupe in 1961. A member of the famous Carter Family, June had been singing on stage since she was 10. She'd seen other country musicians ruin their careers and their lives with drugs.

As Cash sank deeper and deeper into his drug addiction, June realized what was happening and tried to help. To tempt Johnny's appetite, she would cook breakfasts of country ham and biscuits on a tiny grill in the bus as they were traveling.

On stage June covered for him when he wandered in late for a show. When drug pushers came around trying to sell pills to Johnny, June chased them away. She systematically searched for the pills he had hidden in his room and got rid of them. "I don't know why I felt I had the right to do it," she says. "Nobody else would do it. You just can't watch a man kill himself. I couldn't."

In October, 1965, it seemed June had lost the battle. Johnny disappeared. Several days later pictures of

Johnny Cash, handcuffed and escorted by police, appeared in newspapers all across the country. He had been arrested by narcotics agents in El Paso for trying to bring pills across the border from Mexico.

Johnny Cash spent the night in the El Paso jail. The rest of his 30-day sentence was suspended, but he was terribly shaken by the experience. For a month he stayed off pills. But then he slowly drifted back. Soon he was taking as many as before.

After that things went from bad to worse. While driving June's Cadillac one rainy night, Cash rammed a telephone pole, broke his nose, and knocked out 4 teeth. He had to cancel a show in Chicago.

When his wife filed for divorce, Cash became even more depressed. He began missing more and more shows. June Carter and the rest of the troupe, which now included Carl Perkins, the Statler Brothers, and drummer Fluke Holland, worked the dates for him. But often, when Johnny didn't show, the troupe didn't get paid. They were barely making expenses. The Musicians Union threatened to bar Cash.

Turning Point

In 1967, Cash bought a rugged timber and stone house set into a cliff overlooking Old Hickory Lake, near Nashville. It became a refuge for him, and he spent long hours tramping in the surrounding woods, and fishing.

Early one chilly morning in November, Braxton Dixon, who had designed and built Cash's house and had become a good friend, came by to see him. Braxton looked around but couldn't find Johnny. Suddenly he saw Cash's tractor in the lake.

He rushed down, afraid his friend was pinned underneath. Finally he found Cash clinging to a tree, his coat stiff with ice and his face blue. Johnny had jumped clear of the tractor just as it hit the water, but he was too weak to walk back to the house. In another half hour Johnny would have frozen to death.

When June found out about the incident, she told Johnny she was giving up. He begged her to call Nat Winston, a guitar-playing friend who was also a psychiatrist. When Winston arrived, Johnny made June listen while he told the doctor he was going off the pills for good and wanted help. They sensed that this time he meant it.

For the next 2 weeks under Winston's supervision, Cash took fewer pills each day. His friends stayed with him day and night to see him through the terrible withdrawal pains, which Cash describes as the "ragin, screamin' terrors."

After he'd been off the pills for just 3 weeks, Cash went back on tour. Could he stay off drugs this time? The other members of the troupe were doubtful. Dr. Winston had estimated the odds of his shaking the habit after so many years as 3 million to one. But Cash kept his promise. He even went back and made up every show he had missed.

Cash still had to struggle with a continuing craving for drugs. However, before long even Dr. Winston admitted that he had a good chance of winning his battle. "I've never seen anybody come off pills with the guts that John showed," the doctor said. "I have the feeling he's made it . . . I don't think he'll ever have trouble again. I wouldn't make that statement about anybody else I know who has ever been on drugs."

In March, 1969, Johnny Cash and June Carter won a Grammy award for their song, "Jackson." A week later, they were married. Most people thought it was June who had gotten John off drugs. Both of them deny this. "It wasn't even happiness with June that made me do it," says John. "It was *me* that made me do it."

Cash still chuckles at the reaction his comeback produced on Music Row in Nashville. He suspects some people were a little disappointed that he didn't follow country stars Hank Williams and Jimmie Rodgers to an early grave. "Some of them are still mad about it," he says. "I didn't go ahead and die so they'd have a legend to sing about and put me in hillbilly heaven."

Now

In the years since he has been off drugs, Johnny Cash has risen to new heights as a performer. He's played at Carnegie Hall and at the London Palladium. In 1969 his 13-week summer TV show was a smashing success and was rescheduled as a regular weekly program for the next season. A documentary made about his life for educational television was so well received that it was made into a full-length feature film.

How sweet is success to Johnny Cash? "Success is having to worry about everything in the world except money," he grumbles. "I still don't understand it. If you don't have any time for yourself, any time to hunt or fish, that's success."

Why do Cash's songs appeal to so many different types of people? Perhaps it is simply his relentless honesty. No matter what he is singing about or who's in the audience, Johnny Cash insists on "telling it like it is." After his show at San Quentin, a guard observed, "Cash is for real. These cons would spot a phoney in a second."

At his White House concert, President Nixon introduced Johnny Cash as a singer, "not just of country music but of American music that speaks to all Americans." Cash was pleased. He doesn't like people to label his music "country-western." "I just call it Johnny Cash-type music," he says. "I don't imitate anybody."

Cash also gets annoyed when people try to read things into his songs which he feels aren't there. "Most of my songs don't have any deep hidden meanings," he insists. "A few do have a message."

These days, Johnny Cash writes most of his songs at home in his large, oval living room, overlooking Old Hickory Lake. "I generally get an idea for a song every time I'm fishin' or out in the woods," he says. "I write them down after I get home."

The temptation to go back to the pills has faded with time. "Once I would have robbed my mother to get pills," he admits. "Now I can't stand the thought of taking them." Looking back, Cash now feels the pills were an escape. "Maybe I was afraid to face reality," he muses. "I wasn't very happy then. Maybe I was trying to find a spiritual satisfaction in drugs."

Today Cash is still restless, never able to sit still more than a few minutes, relaxed in public only when he is singing. But he seems to have the inner peace he was seeking.

The pressure of concerts and recording is still there,

but Johnny Cash has learned how to handle it. "I feel lately that I'm a smarter man than I was when I was tearing up things," he says. "It was a wild growing up. It's much better now." These days Cash works off tension hoeing corn in his garden.

Occasionally tourist buses rumble by. Sometimes fans stop to chat. "It's good to see you, Johnny. We saw you once at the Iowa State Fair. Can we stand alongside you for a picture, Johnny?" Cash shakes hands and signs autographs good-naturedly. "I love these people," he says. "Seeing those people and letting them see me is where it's at."

Cash plans to keep on traveling — giving concerts in prisons and auditoriums, on reservations and at state fairs. "Television is so impersonal and cold," he explains. "I enjoy personal appearances more than I ever did. When I get to that microphone, I can ramble and feel so free." Road trips aren't so lonely any more. When Cash travels, June and their young son, John Carter, usually come along.

With the exception of Luther Perkins, who died in a tragic fire, all the members of Cash's original group are still with him. Their faith in Johnny during the dark days of his drug addiction has been amply rewarded. Bob Wooton, the young guitarist who took Luther's place, marvels at the group's closeness: "It's like we're all more brothers and sisters than a group of people playing."

We haven't heard the last of Johnny Cash. "Selling a good song is my calling in the world," he says. "There's a lot of songs I haven't sung and a lot of songs to come along. I changed everything. I intend to keep changing. I'm building. I'm expanding. I am still being born. You haven't seen the complete me yet."

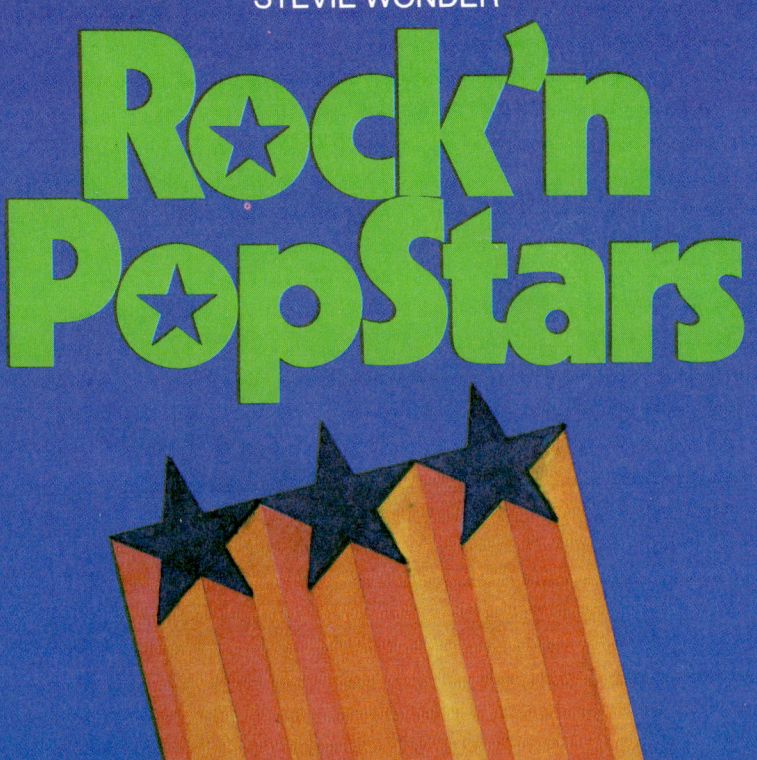